Republican-isms

The Bloopers and Bombast
of the Grand Old Party

COMPILED BY
NICK BAKALAR

ILLUSTRATED BY ROMAN GENN

John Wiley & Sons
New York • Chichester • Brisbane • Toronto • Singapore

For Libby,
who knows sour cream when she sees it

Acknowledgments

Gerry Helferich, who suggested I do this book, is a kind and understanding boss, a knowledgeable and discerning editor, and a loyal friend. How he manages to be all of these things at once, I will never know. I am amazed, honored, and grateful.

Contents

Introduction

> The time comes upon every public man when
> it is best for him to keep his lips closed.
>
> *Abraham Lincoln,* 1860

Republicans say the strangest things, but maybe it's not their fault. After all, politicians have to make speeches for every occasion, express opinions on everything from NAFTA to tomorrow's weather, give their 10-second take on health care or prayer in schools or Bosnia or the price of milk in South Carolina. A politician's got to be ready to have something to say about just about anything, any time. But for these Republicans, that's when the trouble starts—when they open their mouths. On second thought, maybe it really is their fault.

Listen to Bob Dole, telling us what America is "all about": "I don't know, my vision for America is to have a better America… I want a better life for your children. I want a better life, a better life, a better life than we had. We had a better life than our parents, our parents had a better life than their parents. That's what America is all about." Dole suffers from a common Republican disorder: When he talks, his ears stop working.

George Bush is another sufferer, and he's got a worse case. You ask him a question, and you get a response that sounds as if it had been translated into English via Urdu from a Farsi original transcribed by someone whose first language is Cherokee, which he speaks with a Shoshone accent. What else could explain this: "High-tech is potent, precise, and in the end, unbeatable. The truth is, it reminds a lot of people of the way I pitch horseshoes. Would you believe some of the people? Would you believe our dog? Look, I want to give the high-five symbol to high-tech." He's also capable of an incisive remark. "Boy," he marveled during a tour of Auschwitz, "they were big on crematoriums, weren't they?"

Buchanan and Dornan, on the other hand, *can* hear what they're saying. They just don't care. If a man says, as Dornan did, "Every lesbian spear-chucker in the country hopes I get defeated," you're dealing with someone who obviously couldn't care less what he sounds like. Buchanan is much the same: When he says things guaranteed to be offensive to homosexuals, people who believe in evolution, Jews, those who were born in other countries, women, or people who aren't white, you would think he might at least occasionally regret his words, and not say them again. But no. He repeats them, endlessly. The man simply does not give a damn.

For comparison, we have included quotations from some Republican presidents of earlier times. Usually—but not always—they sound a lot better than the current crew. Of course with competition like Forbes, Alexander, Lugar, Keyes, and Gramm, an orator like Dwight Eisenhower starts to sound like Pericles.

Well, here they are—your Republican candidates and ex-candidates, congressmen and senators, governors and presidents, past, present, and presumably future. Read them, and try not to weep, for as George Bush said during the 1992 campaign, "You cannot be president of the United States if you don't have faith. Remember Lincoln, going to his knees in times of trial and the Civil War and all that stuff? You can't be. And we are blessed. So don't feel sorry for—don't cry for me, Argentina."

Bob Dole
Wait! It's My Turn to Be President! Isn't It?

Bob Dole has been getting off a lot of mordant one-liners while waiting to become president. Here are a few of them, along with a few two- and three-liners for good measure.

I didn't want him running out in the street scaring people.

> Why he gave Clinton a contribution toward building a
> White House running track

Stop paying Clinton speech writers by the word.

> On how to shut Clinton up

Sell it.

> On what to do with Arkansas

I slept like a baby. Every two hours I woke up and cried.

> Describing his reaction to his loss in
> New Hampshire in 1988

And we had to have little instructions and little classes on how to conduct a meeting. We never thought we'd be chairmen of anything. So a lot of people were skeptical about me. In any event—so we had these little classes on how to conduct a meeting: how to rap the gavel, how to look straight at the witness while sleeping, and a lot of things.

On learning the techniques of being the majority party in the Senate

The first thing that guy ought to do is get a shave.

Advice to Judge Robert Bork on what to do about his goofy-looking beard

Sort of the ghost of Spiro Agnew.

Description of George Bush, when Bush complained that the press was being hard on him about the Iran-Contra scandal

Hear No Evil, See No Evil, and Evil.

On, respectively, Presidents Ford, Carter, and Nixon

The Chief of Chaff.

On Ronald Reagan's Chief of Staff, John Sununu

A lot of people think I'm grumpy. But you have to remember, my wife's president of the Red Cross. I never know how much blood I gave during the night.

On *The Tonight Show*, 1993

Republicans on Other Republicans
What They Say About Each Other (And Sometimes Right to The Other Guy's Face)

A lot of stuff is said in the heat of battle that isn't really meant, or that will be reconsidered when tempers have cooled and calm reason once again prevails. So quoting these people— especially out of context like this—is, we agree, really not doing justice to these men who only mean the best for each other and for their country. But, you know what? We're doing it anyway.

BUCHANAN ON DOLE: Beltway Bob, the bellhop of the business roundtable.

BUCHANAN ON DOLE: Bob Dole is our Walter Mondale. He's the weakest front-runner I've seen in a long time.

GINGRICH ON DOLE: The tax collector for the welfare state.

He will crack, and people will see he is hollow. There's nothing there. He doesn't have issues. He doesn't debate.

PAT BUCHANAN ON DOLE, *The New York Times,*
March 3, 1996

BUCHANAN ON QUAYLE ON BUCHANAN: Of my speech in Houston, Mr. Quayle writes, "Nobody insisted on clearing Buchanan's text in advance. All Pat had to promise

---

Buchanan Climbs in the Ring with the Republican Heavyweight Tag Team

NEWT GINGRICH ON BUCHANAN: A reactionary, not a conservative. *An upper cut!*

WILLIAM BENNETT ON BUCHANAN: Flirted with fascism. *And a right!*

DAVID FRUM ON BUCHANAN: America's last leftist. *And a left!*

GEORGE F. WILL ON BUCHANAN: A New Deal liberal. *And he's down for the count!*

---

was that in the course of the speech he would endorse the president. [Pat's] tone quickly alienated many in the hall and many more watching at home... Pat just wanted to draw blood and he ended up hurting the president."

But if Dan Quayle believes that, why did he tell CNN's Bernard Shaw, "I thought Pat Buchanan gave a great speech. As a matter of fact, Marilyn and I were talking about it afterward, that was just the kind of speech we had hoped for. Pat Buchanan has the ability to frame the issues. He's a very articulate individual, happens to be a very good friend of ours and he's going to be sitting in the box tonight with Marilyn. So I was there cheering enthusiastically."

These contradictory quotes come from a man who just said of Bill Clinton, Americans "will not tolerate not telling the truth."

(Newspaper column, May 11, 1994)

DOLE ON FORBES: The king of negative advertising.

ALEXANDER ON DOLE AND FORBES: If Steve is the king, Senator Dole is the prince.

ALEXANDER ON BUCHANAN: You're good at what the problem is, but you don't have one single solution.

(Press release, January 4, 1996)

BUCHANAN ON ALEXANDER: The fellow who goes around in the Howdy Doody shirt.

(The New York Times, March 7, 1996)

We're the party of ideas, but that doesn't mean every idea is a good idea. You hear Gingrich's staff has these five file

---

And Now, Ladies and Gentlemen, for the Lightweight Championship of Downtown Columbia, South Carolina: Lamar Alexander vs. Steve Forbes

ALEXANDER ON FORBES [commenting on an anti-Alexander TV ad]: Steve, you haven't learned a single thing in your whole campaign. You should be ashamed of yourself.

FORBES ON ALEXANDER: That was a charitable ad—that ad did not talk about some of those cozy business deals you did as Governor.

ALEXANDER ON FORBES: You should go practice your dirty business on a race for the school board before you try for the Presidency of the United States.

(Debate, Columbia South Carolina, February 29, 1996)

---

cabinets, four big ones, and one little tiny one. No. 1. Is "Newt's Ideas," No. 2 is "Newt's Ideas," No. 3, No. 4 "Newt's Ideas." The little one is "Newt's Good Ideas."

BOB DOLE on Newt's good and bad ideas, 1995

What you have here is an Administration that has set its hair on fire and is trying to put it out with a hammer.

AL D'AMATO, Republican senator from New York, on Reagan administration policy in Panama, 1988

DOLE ON **R**EAGAN: A programmed line reader… [His] mind is primitive… [He] thinks in slogans. A befuddled septuagenarian.

DOLE ON **B**USH: He screws with his socks on.

DOLE ON **Q**UAYLE: Mr. Potato Head.

DOLE ON **K**EMP: There's a certain football player who forgot his helmet and then started talking supply-side theory.

In a recent fire, Bob Dole's library burned down. Both books were lost. And he hadn't even finished coloring one of them yet.

JACK KEMP, 1985

Dare Not Speak
Its Name
Republicans and Gay People

Gay people aren't going to find many friends among the current crop of Republicans. And they'll stay far away from Bob Dornan and Pat Buchanan, if they know what's good for them. Buchanan feels he's at war with them; Dornan thinks God doesn't like them as much as He likes Bob Dornan.

The poor homosexuals—they have declared war on nature, and now nature is exacting an awful retribution.

PAT BUCHANAN on AIDS, 1983

It was not the right that suddenly began issuing ultimatums on society. It was not the right that started this cultural war. It was the militant homosexuals who first stormed across society's old borders. And it is they who are assaulting traditional positions while painting themselves as victims of social and legal persecution.

PAT BUCHANAN, newspaper column, September 14, 1994

The cause of this cultural war then, is the relentless drive by homosexuals and their allies to use schools and media to validate and propagate their moral beliefs, to convert all of America to those beliefs, and to codify them in federal law.

PAT BUCHANAN, newspaper column, September 14, 1994

Americans are a tolerant people. But a majority believes that the sexual practices of gays, whether a result of nature or nurture, are both morally wrong and medically ruinous. Many consider this "reactionary" or "homophobic." But our beliefs are rooted in the Old and New Testament, in natural law and tradition, even in the writing of that paragon of the Enlightenment, Thomas Jefferson (who felt homosexuality should be punished as severely as rape).

PAT BUCHANAN, newspaper column, September 14, 1994

Thirty years ago, both sides in today's cultural war shared the belief that homosexuals, be they 2 or 10 percent of the population, had the same constitutional rights as the rest of us, as well as a right to be let alone. We still do. Homosexuality was not an issue then. What makes it an issue now is the non-negotiable demand that this "lifestyle" be sanctioned by law, that gays be granted equal rights to marry, adopt and serve as troop leaders in the Boy Scouts. Let me be blunt: We can't support this.

To force it upon us is like forcing Christians to burn incense to the emperor.

PAT BUCHANAN, campaign position paper, 1996

The party of homosexuals.

ORRIN HATCH, Republican senator from Utah,
describing the Democratic Party

But if a person is still living a lifestyle that is an offense to God, there's no room to recognize them in our party... I hope my party never officially recognizes groups that are based upon observable offenses against God and the natural order.

BOB DORNAN, commenting on the Log Cabin Club,
an organization of gay Republicans

Funny Clothes
and Foreign Accents
Republicans and
the Immigrants

The culture war is on, and Republicans are armed to the teeth. Contractors all over the country are getting ready to bid on Pat Buchanan's Great Wall of the Rio Grande, and governors of every border state are planning how to spend that windfall they're going to get when they no longer have to send illegal immigrants' children to elementary school. As long as these guys are around, America has nothing to fear from inferior people anywhere.

I think there is a broad consensus in this country to stop the inflow of illegal aliens and to stop subsidizing illegal aliens by paying them, putting them on welfare.

NEWT GINGRICH, *This Week With David Brinkley,* January 2, 1994

Illegal immigration must be halted, and no illegal alien given welfare. We need a nationwide Proposition 187, a closing of the Southwest border to illegals (with the National Guard, if necessary) and a new immigration law where we Americans decide who comes, and when. Our first concern must be the peace, stability and unity of our own country.

PAT BUCHANAN, campaign position paper, 1996

I don't know much about Americanism, but it's a damn good word with which to carry an election.

WARREN G. HARDING

Other People, Other Lands: Two Republican Views

I am not here to talk surrender terms, but to talk about how to fight and win the cultural war for the soul of our country. Our culture is superior. Our culture is superior because our religion is Christianity and that is the truth that makes men free.

PAT BUCHANAN, speaking at the Christian Coalition annual conference, 1993

Any man who tries to excite class hatred, sectional hatred, hatred of creeds, any kind of hatred in our community, though he may affect to do it in the interest of the class he is addressing, is in the long run with absolute certainty that class's own worst enemy.

THEODORE ROOSEVELT, address in Omaha, Nebraska, May 27, 1903

Dan Quayle Quiz

Take out your pencils—it's quiz time! Each of the following multiple choice questions begins with an actual Dan Quayle quote, but only one of the four phrases that follows is the correct ending. Answers below. No peeking.

1. I love California. I practically grew up in: Ⓐ Ⓑ Ⓒ Ⓓ

a. a part of Los Angeles, but really outside Los Angeles's inside part.

b. San Francisco, which is to the north of Los Angeles.

c. Phoenix.

d. the pro shop at the Pebble Beach Golf Course.

2. I am not the problem. I am: Ⓐ Ⓑ Ⓒ Ⓓ

a. only a large part of the problem.

b. a Republican.

c. not the solution, either.

d. going to solve the problem if I understand it.

3. If we don't succeed, we run the risk of: Ⓐ Ⓑ Ⓒ Ⓓ

a. a large mortgage payment.

b. failure.

c. trying again.

d. paying the price of expensive foreign vegetables.

4. We're going to have:

a. the best educated American people in the world.

b. the best Americans in the educated world.

c. the best world the best educated American people can have.

d. the whole educated world watching the Olympics in Atlanta on TV.

5. Mars is:

a. a small little big planet, and a red one, too.

b. somewhat the same distance from the Sun, which is very important.

c. somewhat important, but not as important as tort reform.

d. a heck of a long way from here, that's for sure.

6. Republicans understand the importance of:

a. bondage between a parent and child.

b. discipline to raise children from bondage.

c. bondage and discipline.

d. raising bonded American children.

7. I was interested in joining the National Guard because: (A) (B) (C) (D)

a. in the summer they have a whole keg of beer on Saturdays.

b. it enabled me to go to law school as soon as possible.

c. it enabled me to serve my country and yet be home every evening.

d. it was a good idea at that time, even though you don't think so now.

8. Desert Storm was a stirring victory for:

a. the forces of aggression and lawlessness.

b. the disloyal doubters and do-gooders.

c. the good guys over some really bad guys.

d. Barbara and for President Bush, too.

9. Vietnam was a jungle... Kuwait, Iraq, Saudi Arabia:

a. you have heat, but it's a dry heat.

b. are in the Far East, way out there.

c. they've got almost no trees at all, some palm trees maybe.

d. you have sand.

10. We are ready:

a. for any unforeseen event that may or may not occur.

b. for things that might happen and might not, depending.

c. for anything that will happen, but probably won't.

d. for dinner.

Answers: 1c. 2b. 3b. 4a. 5b. 6a. 7b. 8a. 9d. 10a.

Onward and Upward with the Arts

When they're not reading Yeats, Republicans go to the movies a lot, and they listen to music, too. They watch TV endlessly. And they go to museums and art galleries. But we'll tell you something: Except for liking Walt Disney, and recognizing that he was a Great American, they don't like what they're seeing, and they don't like what they're hearing! Not one bit!

Yet, today, America's culture—movies, television, magazines, music—is polluted with lewdness and violence. Museums and art galleries welcome exhibits that mock our patriotism and our faith... This campaign to malign America's heroes and defile America's past has as its end: To turn America's children against what their parents believe and what they love.

PAT BUCHANAN, announcement speech, March 20, 1995

It is essential to understand why *The Killing Fields* had rave reviews from left-wing intellectuals, while *Rambo* was laughed at: *Rambo* was overtly anti-Communist, while *The Killing Fields* managed to somehow pin the blame on

America for what was clearly a Communist genocidal action in Cambodia.

NEWT GINGRICH, speech in Congress, 1986

One story after another, whether it is taking that Italian classic, *Pinocchio*, or a British classic like *Peter Pan*, he took the past works, added to his own creations, and has given us a timeless legacy where, centuries from now when everybody is forgotten in this House—and I know the President would not mind my saying even Ronald Reagan retreating to a few paragraphs—they will be adding more stereophonic sound quality, more Dolby sound quality and more color enhancement and probably three dimensions to all of these works of Walt Disney... Walt Disney Recognition Day. What a Joy!

BOB DORNAN speaking in favor of a piece of legislation he sponsored to designate December 5, 1986, as Walt Disney Recognition Day, *The Congressional Record*, August 8, 1986

I'm... going to see it [Oliver Stone's *Nixon*] and from what I have read about it, it is a disgrace to the name of Walt Disney, who was a great American.

PAT BUCHANAN, CNN interview, December 26, 1995 (The film *Nixon* was produced by the Disney Company.)

I'm all for Lawrence Welk. Lawrence Welk is a wonderful man. He used to be, or was, or—wherever he is now, bless him.

> **GEORGE BUSH**, trying to remember whether Lawrence Welk was dead or alive at the time, February 16, 1989

Slouching Towards Washington

Both Patrick Buchanan and Robert Dornan have apparently been reading William Butler Yeats in their spare time. We know of no rational explanation for this.

You know, W.B. Yeats once said, "Things reveal themselves passing away." And the establishment of the Republican Party, in its frenzy, in its horror, in the names it is calling me, is holding up a mirror to itself, not to me, and I would say that with reference to Senator D'Amato.

PAT BUCHANAN, *The New York Times*, March 3, 1996

My favorite poet, William B. Yeats, wrote these words in 1939, the year Hitler began the world's most devastating war: "Things fall apart. The center cannot hold. The blood-dimmed tide is loosed. And everywhere the ceremony of innocence is drowned. The best lack all conviction and the worst are full of passionate intensity."

ROBERT DORNAN, announcement speech, April 13, 1995

The first thing we should do is eliminate the National Endowments for the Arts and Humanities. Why is the Federal government in the culture business? And, in this explosion of the information age, why do we have a Corporation for Public Broadcasting?

BOB DOLE, announcement speech, April 11, 1995

My friends, if there is room in America for the fighting song of the civil rights movement, *We Shall Overcome*, then there's got to be room for *Dixie* as well.

PAT BUCHANAN, February 29, 1996

Shame is a powerful tool. We should use it. So, together, let's refocus the spotlight. Let's put the heat on the entertainment industry. Society pays a steep price when the entertainment industry poisons the minds of our young people. We must hold Hollywood accountable for putting profit ahead of common decency.

BOB DOLE, announcement speech, April 11, 1995

27

Bang, Bang, You're Dead
Republicans and Guns

Not all of them actually love guns the way Pat Buchanan and Newt Gingrich apparently do. But they certainly seem to like them a lot. Bob Dole has a warm correspondence with the National Rifle Association, an excerpt from which appears below.

I won't support gun control because the only people it's going to affect are middle-class law-abiding citizens. If we lock up all the violent criminals and we have enough prisons built and that doesn't work, then I'm prepared to look at gun control.

> **NEWT GINGRICH**, interview with David Brinkley, January 2, 1994

As long as there are guns, the individual that wants a gun for a crime is going to have one and going to get it. The only person who's going to be penalized and have difficulty is the law-abiding citizen, who then cannot have it if he wants protection—the protection of a weapon in his home, for home protection.

> **RONALD REAGAN**

Gun control is a completely ineffective approach to the lack of safety and security in our communities. Disarming law-abiding citizens only places them at the mercy of those who break the law. Again, I enjoyed our visit and look forward to continuing to work with you and the membership of the National Rifle Association on the concerns we share.

BOB DOLE, letter to the NRA, March 10, 1995

I come from a state where gun control is just how steady you hold your weapon.

ALAN SIMPSON, Republican senator from
Wyoming, 1991

He Said That?

Every once in a while, something uncharacteristic comes out of Republicans' mouths. Here are some samples.

If you're looking for ideology—well, there's Ronald Reagan. Then you see how the debt went up during those years.

BOB DOLE, 1995

He [Jimmy Carter] is without a doubt the most consistent citizen of our former Presidents. If you watch him, you get a little shamed into being a better citizen yourself.

NEWT GINGRICH, to his class at Kennesaw State College, November 28, 1993

Everything ought to be based on potential. Everyone should be treated alike, whether they're black or brown or disabled or homosexual.

BOB DOLE

I think the press has, overall, been very tough on the President and on Mrs. Clinton.

NEWT GINGRICH, *Meet the Press*, NBC October 2, 1994

I'm trying to impress my Republican friends that we are not anti-people. We Republicans are always reacting to these programs. It seems time now for us to be responsive to people who are eligible and who are not being adequately served.

BOB DOLE

The greatest leaders in fighting for an integrated America in the twentieth century were in the Democratic Party. The fact is, it was the liberal wing of the Democratic Party that ended segregation. The fact is that it was Franklin Delano Roosevelt who gave hope to a nation that was in despair and could have slid into dictatorship. And the fact is, every Republican has much to learn from studying what Democrats did right.

NEWT GINGRICH , first speech as
Speaker of the House 1995

Someone else is going to have to start taking hits besides welfare recipients.

BOB DOLE, in a conversation with Ronald Reagan, 1981

I'll be glad to reply to or dodge your questions, depending on what I think will help our election most.

GEORGE BUSH in an uncharacteristic flash of wit
during the 1980 presidential campaign

Civilization and Its Malcontents
Family Values, Etc.

Here are the Republicans on the profound issues that matter most to Americans: family values, hard work, moral vision, hope, truth, faith, the rule of law, James Bond, and how voting Republican will prevent mothers from killing their children. If you really care, America, read on.

People like me are what stand between us and Auschwitz. I see evil around me every day.

> **NEWT GINGRICH**, *The Atlanta Journal and Constitution*, January 1994

James Bond is a man of honor, a symbol of real value to the free world.

> **RONALD REAGAN**, 1983

America is in crying need of the moral vision you have brought to our political life… What great goals you have!

> **GEORGE BUSH** to Jerry Falwell, 1987

I mean a child that doesn't have a parent to read to that child or that doesn't see that when the child is hurting to have a parent and help out or neither parent there enough to pick the kid up and dust him off and send him back into the game at school or whatever, that kid has a disadvantage.

GEORGE BUSH, elucidating his theory of child rearing, 1992

I personally favor mandatory requirement of work for everybody, including women with young children.

NEWT GINGRICH, *Renewing American Civilization* lecture series

The mother killing the two children in South Carolina vividly reminds every American how sick the society is getting and how much we need to change things. The only way you get change is to vote Republican.

NEWT GINGRICH, November 1994

The Law

No man is above the law and no man is below it; nor do we ask any man's permission when we require him to obey it. Obedience to the law is demanded as a right; not asked as a favor.

THEODORE ROOSEVELT, Third Annual Message, December 7, 1903

When the President does it, that means it's not illegal.

RICHARD NIXON, 1974

R.GENN

It's Not An Easy Life
Being a Republican

It is a major, major mistake we've made since World War II to suggest that life is easy and the difficulties are the aberration. I think the opposite is true. I think life is normally hard, and it's the good moments that are the aberration. And that you work hard and you try to raise a family and you try to earn a living and you try to have a safe neighborhood precisely for the good moments. But that a healthy society starts out saying: Life is hard.

NEWT GINGRICH from a tape he made called *History and Leadership*, quoted in *The Washington Post*, December 19, 1994

I wish to preach, not the doctrine of ignoble ease, but the doctrine of the strenuous life.

THEODORE ROOSEVELT, speech before the Hamilton Club, Chicago, April 10, 1889

Does that mean I have to get up?

RONALD REAGAN, quoted by Michael Deaver, who awakened him at 9 A.M. on Inauguration Day 1981, and told him that he was to be sworn in in two hours

Education
You May Be a Monkey's Nephew, but I'm Certainly Not

Republicans are highly interested in education. They have put forward various ideas, but the ones they all agree on are: pray in school, study your Bible, and get rid of the Department of Education "as soon as I'm elected." Pat Buchanan, who seems particularly interested in our schools, holds some unusual beliefs about evolution and the theory of natural selection, and he's certainly got a problem with Jonathan Kozol.

You may believe you're descended from monkeys; I don't believe it. I think you're descended, I think you're a creature of God... I believe that God created heaven and earth. I believe, first, I believe the literal New Testament is literally the word of God, and I believe the Old Testament is the inspired word of God... I think they have a right to insist that Godless evolution not be taught to their children or their children not be indoctrinated in it.

PAT BUCHANAN, February 1996

To equalize expenditures among all public schools would entail a transfer of scores of billions of dollars from taxpayers to a public school system that ought to be reformed or jettisoned, not enriched… Money is not the big problem, though it is the big agenda item of Jonathan Kozol and the educational *banditi* cheering him on… When we introduce into classrooms the competitive ethos we see on our athletic fields, we will win there as we win in the Olympics. Not before "A little less Jonathan Kozol, please, and a little more Vince Lombardi."

PAT BUCHANAN, newspaper column, September 1991

And how can we ever again succeed in educating children to become moral men and women if, in America's public schools, we consciously deny them all religious instruction, and deny them access to that primary source of morality, God's own word. The Bible is the one book from which they are expressly not allowed to be taught.

PAT BUCHANAN, speech, May 6, 1995

But today, in too many of our schools our children are being robbed of their innocence. Their minds are being poisoned against their Judeo-Christian heritage, against America's heroes and against American history, against the values of faith and family and country.

PAT BUCHANAN, announcement speech, March 20, 1995

I walk into a classroom, talk as a presidential candidate to the great issues of the day and then spend the first twenty minutes answering questions from the assembled wholesome, young people of northern New Hampshire about "gay marriages" and homosexuality. We have turned our schools over to people who are now directing our children to obsess about their perverse, sexual lusts and all we want to do is talk about the balanced budget and the flat tax.

ALAN KEYES, February 26, 1996

Changing Times on the Educational Scene

Aid to education in the states by the Nation seems to be our best chance to bring up the neglected elements in our population.

RUTHERFORD B. HAYES, 1884

We should put an end to the entire process. The federal government should have no role in primary and secondary education.

PAT BUCHANAN, May 16, 1995

The Quiet Pleasures of Self-Pity

Feeling sorry for yourself is a big part of any political campaign.
The Republicans can be just as pitiful as the Democrats when
they want to be.

I won't buy it because as I stood up for conservatism in all
these years, as I stood up to be vilified by Black liberals and
called a traitor to my race, as I paid my dues and took my
licks, I didn't do it for the sake of representing the view
that government protectionism or government socialism
is the answer to America's problems.

ALAN KEYES, February 25, 1996

I've been told that my campaign for President is at a disadvantage because many believe I have the most experience
and expertise in leading national security and foreign policy, subjects in which supposedly there is little voter interest.

RICHARD LUGAR, announcement speech, April 19, 1995

I mention all of this because I have been asked repeatedly by members of the national media about a quality
called "charisma." The pointed suggestion of the pundits
is that a charisma deficiency may be just as fatal to an

aspiring politician as a vitamin deficiency may be to any human being.

RICHARD LUGAR, speech to the Christian Coalition, September 8, 1995

This year, we've had one traditional Catholic running for president for the Republican Party for the first time, one African-American, and one Jewish-American, and Senator D'Amato and his legal folks have tried to keep all three of us off the ballot in New York.

PAT BUCHANAN, *The New York Times*, March 3, 1996

I want you to know who I am, because I'm not here to ask for anybody's pity, but I want you to know who Bob Dole is...

BOB DOLE, *The New York Times*, March 8, 1996

I plead guilty to being a capitalist.

LAMAR ALEXANDER, defending an insider investment deal he took advantage of when he was Governor of Tennessee

Contrast this self-indulgence and self-pity with the spirit of the forgotten heroes of 1776, the men who pledged "lives, fortunes and sacred honor" to defend their Declaration of Independence.

PAT BUCHANAN, introduction to the "Library" section of his home page on the World Wide Web

Could I Re-Phrase That Last Statement? Please?

Every once in a while—well, several times a day, actually—Republicans will say something they later regret, and a lot of times they say things they probably should regret, but don't. Here are some examples from both categories.

The central objection to the present flood of illegals is they are not English-speaking white people from Western Europe; they are Spanish-speaking brown and black people from Mexico, Latin America, and the Caribbean.

PAT BUCHANAN, newspaper column, 1990

Boy, they were big on crematoriums, weren't they?

GEORGE BUSH on a tour of Auschwitz,
September 28, 1987

The Congress will push me to raise taxes, and I'll say no, and they'll push, and I'll say no, and they'll push again. And all I can say to them is, "Read my lips: No new taxes."

BUSH, 1988 acceptance speech

Maybe the Things
Senator Alfonse D' Amato
Says and Does in Public Make Him Sound Cruder, Stupider, and More Vulgar Than He Actually Is. Or, on the Other Hand, Maybe Not.

President Clinton had a bill, e-i-e-i-o. And in that bill was lots of pork, e-i-e-i-o.

AL D'AMATO, who actually *sang* these words to the tune of "Old MacDonald Had a Farm" on the floor of the Senate in full view of spectators and C-Span cameras, which recorded the event, video and sound, for the ages.

Judge Ito loves the limelight. He is making a disgrace of the judicial system. Little Judge Ito. For God's sake... get this thing over. I mean this is a disgrace. Judge Ito with the wet nose. And then he's going to have a hung jury. Judge Ito will keep us from getting television for the next year.

AL D'AMATO, in yet another failed attempt at wit, speaking in a slapstick Asian accent on Don Imus's talk radio show, 1995

With 80,000 dead of AIDS, 3,000 more buried each month, our promiscuous homosexuals appear literally hell-bent on Satanism and suicide.

PAT BUCHANAN, 1990

Masochism and sadism and other perverted sex practices are, in many instances, the result of demon possession.

PAT ROBERTSON, *Answers to 200 of Life's Most Probing Questions*

Biology and History with Professors Coolidge and Buchanan, First Semester

America must be kept American. Biological laws show… that Nordics deteriorate when mixed with other races.

CALVIN COOLIDGE, 1921

Why are we more shocked when a dozen people are killed in Vilnius than by a massacre in Burundi? Because they are white people. That's who we are. That's where America comes from.

PAT BUCHANAN, 1991

I cannot for the life of me think of any reason in the world why I would want to meet with a congregation of baby butchers. I hate to think what you might be serving for breakfast.

> **JACK WELLBORN**, Congressman from Michigan, responding to a breakfast invitation from a provider of abortion services in his district

If I could find a way to get him out of there, even putting a contract out on him, if the CIA did that sort of thing, assuming it ever did, I would be for it.

> **RICHARD NIXON**, telling George Bush how to take care of the Saddam Hussein problem, 1991

What's wrong with being a boring kind of guy? I think to kind of suddenly try to get my hair colored, dance up and down in a miniskirt or do something to show I've got a lot of jazz out there and drop a bunch of one-liners… We're talking about the President of the United States. This is serious business.

> **GEORGE BUSH**

Capital punishment is our society's recognition of the sanctity of human life.

> **ORRIN HATCH**, Republican senator from Utah, 1988

It's no exaggeration to say the undecideds could go one way or the other.

GEORGE BUSH, campaign rally, October 21, 1988

If we added up all the killed and wounded in Democrat wars in this century, it would be about 1.6 million Americans, enough to fill the city of Detroit.

BOB DOLE, debating Walter Mondale, October 1976

Bob Dornan
B-1 Bob, the Big Brave
Slightly Wacky Fighter Pilot

Almost every chance he gets, Bob Dornan will tell you about the homosexual threat to America. And the threat of drugs, sex, bestiality, public television, prostitution, Bill Clinton, Satan, perverts, abortion, draft-dodgers, Madonna, adultery, the National Endowment for the Arts, communists, Ted Kennedy...

You can get elected by proclaiming that you are a sodomite and engage in anal sex all the time. You will get elected.

The Congressional Record, October 19, 1990

Every lesbian spear-chucker in this country is hoping I get defeated.

The Los Angeles Times, October 18, 1990

Think of the NEA, art funding for perverts and sodomites, putting on filthy stage shows across the country. The latest grants have no strings attached. They are going to write crummy, rotten, blasphemous material and are going to have these $8,000 grants to buy their groceries while they defile and further pollute the American public marketplace.

The Congressional Record, November 6, 1991

In other words, it is a nightmare, and they are not briefing the Congress who pays for all this and recruits these people and they have no policy and the Commander-in-Chief [Clinton] is jogging in San Francisco in his slit-up-the-sides silk girlie-girlie jogging pants showing us those beautiful white doughboy thighs of his.

The Congressional Record, October 6, 1993

And if you want an up or down vote on NEA, a pro-NEA vote is going to be interpreted, and I'll make sure it is, on November 6 as a vote for child pornography, a vote for blaspheming our Lord and Savior Jesus Christ, and a vote for defending the Hollywood left.

The Congressional Record, July 25, 1990

Bob Dornan Wants to Know

How many people are going to emulate now, trying to go to high school like Sharon Stone, with no underwear on because she uncrossed her legs in front of five detectives?

BOB DORNAN, *Showbiz Today,* CNN, June 1, 1992

Please do not write or call us at *Republican-isms.*
Instead, contact Congressman Robert K. Dornan
directly with your response. Operators are standing by.

These are either women trapped in men's bodies, like Alan Alda or Phil Donahue, or younger guys who are like camp followers looking for easy sex.

On men in the pro-choice movement, *The Los Angeles Times,* February 10, 1990

It is a disloyal, treasonous act to use illegal substances in this country, and let us get that clear.

The Congressional Record, January 28, 1992

I look at Madonna in her see-through red panties and bra, wrapped in the American flag on MTV starting yesterday, telling people to vote, and I think how can we have a young generation going in such opposite directions. How can we ever convince young people that it is wrong, that it is naughty to smoke marijuana cigarettes…?

The Congressional Record, October 21, 1990

If America is a sick society, and we sure have a war on our hands, Mr. Speaker, it is because we drink daily at the polluted waters of a popular culture into which Hollywood—that is, left-wing Hollywood, these days—and an artistic *avant-garde* continue to dump their filth. Cleanup time. Yes, the Hollywood left is out there hyping for the Big Green, a proposition in California to clean up the physical environment, but meanwhile they have polluted the spiritual and moral climate of our country.

The Congressional Record, October 19, 1990

The dominant media culture, Mr. Speaker, does not believe adultery counts. That is, of course, a Hollywood deeply held belief—the Hollywood left, that is. And the liberal left of course does not care about draft dodging at all. The liberal media dweebs just about all dogged it during the Korean and Vietnamese fighting. Just check out dominant media culture executives in their mid-forties to mid-fifties and ask their branch of service. You'll get a long stare, and the rare exception proves the rule. They didn't go to Vietnam or NATO and, by the way, only four percent ever go to church.

The Congressional Record, August 5, 1992

Bob Dornan Is Hearing Things

I, personally, can hear a faint bugle call echoing down through 210 years of American history, a challenge. A challenge that calls out to all Americans, "Defend your homeland, defend the West, defend Judeo-Christian ethical standards, defend Western civilization, defend liberty."

The Congressional Record, October 14, 1986

If They Hate Washington and the Government So Much, How Come They All Want to Live in Washington and Be in the Government?

Steve Forbes and Alan Keyes can make a virtue of their lack of experience—in fact, Forbes never misses a chance to do so, and he repeatedly tells people that he's not a Washington insider, even though no one, so far as we know, has ever accused him of being one. Pat Buchanan's self-justification in this matter, below, seems particularly ingenious. Anyway, this is another of those things they all agree on: Government stinks, and so does Washington.

I think all of us realize, if Washington insiders had the answers, they would have implemented them by now.

STEVE FORBES, speech, October 23, 1995

They've been in Washington too long. They talk Washington. They think Washington.

LAMAR ALEXANDER, on Dole and Gramm, *The New York Times*, February 1996

And they do this all in the guise of compassion. It reminds me of that old saying that the ten most frightening words in the English language are "I'm from the Government and I'm here to help you."

STEVE FORBES, campaign position paper, 1996

I am in Washington, not of it. No insider challenges an incumbent president. That makes me, *de facto*, an outsider.

PAT BUCHANAN, 1992

Lamar's out there every day claiming he's the outsider. I remember meeting him when I came to Washington.

BOB DOLE, 1995

Voice in the Wilderness:

Yes, the federal government is big, but the federal government does a lot of good things.

BOB DOLE, August 13, 1995

Good Neighbors
and
Good Fences

One truth must rule all we think and all we do. No people can live to itself alone. The unity of all who dwell in freedom is their only true defense. The economic need of all nations—in mutual dependence—makes isolation an impossibility; not even America's prosperity could long survive if other nations did not prosper. No nation can longer be a fortress, alone and strong and safe. And any people seeking such shelter for themselves can now build only their own prison.

DWIGHT EISENHOWER, Second Inaugural Address, January 1957

I will stop this massive illegal immigration cold. Period. Paragraph. I'll build that security fence, and we'll close it, and we'll say, "Listen José, you're not coming in!"

PATRICK BUCHANAN, *The New York Times*, March 3, 1996

Our Friends in Foreign Lands

Mexicans with their illegal immigrants, Canadians and their bilingual jabbering, Egyptians and Israelis dressing funny and taking our money, South America with all those little separate individual countries, the United Nations where half the time they don't even speak English for God's sake—let's face it, we'd be better off without the whole lot of them. At least that's the way Pat Buchanan seems to see it. So do the other Republicans, though in varying degrees.

Now, Egypt and Israel are friends. But we do friends no favor by putting them on the welfare rolls, which is what foreign aid is. It creates dependency, breeds corruption, corrodes honest relations, and bloats government at the expense of the private sector.

PAT BUCHANAN, December 21, 1994

I didn't go down there with any plan for the Americas, or anything. I went down there to find out from them and their views. You'd be surprised. They're all individual countries.

RONALD REAGAN, on Latin America, 1982

R.GLENN

The point I'm making is that there are losers in the go-go, global economy, friends. There are losers from these trade deals, as well as winners. And someone in this country has got to speak up for the folks who have lost here. It's our country, my friends. We are the true sons and daughters of the Founding Fathers, and we are coming to take repossession of our father's house.

PAT BUCHANAN in *The New York Times*, February 29, 1996

We must have adequate professional forces to impose our will on the Third World. Let me repeat that, because it is a very unfashionable thing to say. There are those moments in life when we are going to disagree with other people, and it is my belief that when we fundamentally disagree with someone, we should win.

NEWT GINGRICH, 1980

We must stop placing the agenda of the United Nations before the interests of the United States. When we take our revolution to the White House in 1996, we will vow that American policies will be determined by us, not by the United Nations. Let us remember that America has been the greatest force for good the world has ever known.

BOB DOLE, 1995

Lost Causes

We all have our distant hopes and unrealized dreams—it's just that most of us don't get to publish them in the paper every morning. Lamar Alexander hopes he can explain how the Republicans' platform adds up to hope. Bob Dole hopes Steve Forbes will defend him. Richard Lugar hopes someone will listen to him. Mock if you will, but this section is their memorial.

I was thinking that maybe if while the Congress and the president are in Washington at loggerheads, they would pass a law cutting their own pay while they can't agree on the budget, it will speed things up just a little bit. I think when they're out of work, when they can't do their job, they ought not to be paid. That might be a good way to start things off.

> **LAMAR ALEXANDER**, *The New York Times*,
> February, 1996

Steve, you've got to defend me. Someone has to defend me.

> **BOB DOLE** to Steve Forbes, during a debate with him and
> other candidates, February 29, 1996

Well, Senator, you've been on the payroll for 35 years; if you can't defend yourself now, I can't help you.

> **STEVE FORBES**, to Bob Dole, in response to Dole's
> appeal, February 29, 1996

Nobody wants to talk about nuclear terrorism, but hiding from it won't make it go away.

RICHARD LUGAR, *The New York Times*, February, 1996

Well there is going to be a need for inspiration, too. We are going to have to explain how balanced-budget amendments and orphanages, and doing away with school lunch programs and racial preferences—how all that adds up to hope.

LAMAR ALEXANDER, illuminating Republican strategy for the 1996 election campaign, 1995

The Richard Lugar Tax Plan: If There Are Any Tax Loopholes Left After I Abolish Taxes, I'll Abolish Them, Too

Specifically, I propose to abolish completely the federal individual and corporate income taxes, capital gains taxes, gift taxes, and inheritance taxes all at the same time. And with them all of the tax loopholes which have been created for special interests.

RICHARD LUGAR, announcement speech, April, 19, 1995

Talking About Yourself in the Third Person

Politicians—and not just Republicans—are always talking about themselves as if they were someone else. Nobody else we know ever does this. Can anyone explain?

I can't promise that Alan Keyes will be the next president of the United States, but I can promise that we're going to raise the standard high in this country…

ALAN KEYES, *The New York Times*, February 1996

Bob Dole is a conservative who gets things done.

BOB DOLE

Bob Dornan will probably never retire.

BOB DORNAN, announcement speech,
April 13, 1995

The conventional wisdom of generous columnists seems to be that Dick Lugar would be a good President. That he is intelligent, has broad experience, exercises courage and prudence appropriately.

DICK LUGAR, announcement speech, April 19, 1995

Statement of Congressman Bob Dornan from California: Homosexuals are notoriously promiscuous, period, fact.

BOB DORNAN, *The Congressional Record*, March 11, 1993

Clearly, there is tremendous movement behind Buchanan that is not only inside the Republican Party…

PAT BUCHANAN, *The New York Times*, March 7, 1996

The only one authorized to make a statement about where this campaign is going is Steve Forbes.

STEVE FORBES, *The New York Times*, March 12, 1996

So that's what Bob Dole is all about.

BOB DOLE, *The New York Times*, March 8, 1996

Who better to talk to a tax increase to death than Jack Kemp.

JACK KEMP, 1989

R.GENN

Pat Buchanan
The Republican They Won't Let Use the Swimming Pool

Why's Everybody Always Picking on Me?

In this campaign, I have been called an anti-Semite, a homophobe, a racist, a sexist, a nativist, a protectionist, an isolationist, a social fascist, and a beer-hall conservative. And then Sam Donaldson had the nerve to ask me on the Brinkley show if I was insensitive, too.

During the 1992 Presidential campaign

Fearless Pat Buchanan Takes on the Controversial Issues of Our Day(And With Devastating Sarcasm)

They took Washington's name off Washington's birthday. It is now President's Day so we can all pay homage to Millard Fillmore, Franklin Pierce, and Bill Clinton. When I get up there, it will be Washington's Birthday all over again, folks.

Speech to Ross Perot's United We Stand, 1995

Maybe It's Something You Said, Pat.

Something is terribly amiss when we can be caught up in remorse over crimes committed in Eastern Europe four decades ago while overlooking the Holocaust going on within our own land, with 4,000 children being done to death every single day.

Newspaper column, 1990

Homosexuality is not a civil right. Its rise is almost always accompanied, as in the Weimar Republic, with a decay of

---

Pat Buchanan & Goldman, Sachs:

...I read a story from New York about 58 new partners made at Goldman, Sachs, each of whom had gotten a bonus of at least $5 million that year.

Announcement speech, March 20, 1995

That is the authentic voice of Goldman, Sachs, and, regrettably, of our own Republican elites.

Campaign position paper, 1996

To ship Mexico tens of billions to pay off its bondholders at Citibank and Goldman, Sachs, President Clinton had to act by executive order.

Campaign position paper, 1996

society and a collapse of its basic cinder block, the family … A visceral recoil from homosexuality is the natural reaction of a healthy society wishing to preserve itself.

Newspaper column, 1991

We're going to go up to that big Republican country club and demand admission. We're going to use the swimming pool and everything else.

The New York Times, March 4, 1996

Mysteriously Linked?

Politicians of both parties sold us out up in Washington, DC. They took Citibank, Chase Manhattan, J.P. Morgan, and Goldman, Sachs off the hook…

Speech in Dallas, August 12, 1995

The GOP is acting less like a great party than like the political action committee of Goldman, Sachs.

Campaign position paper, 1996

Newly installed President Ernesto Zedillo said he needed the cash to pay off bonds held by Citibank and Goldman, Sachs, lest the New World Order come crashing down…

Campaign position paper, 1996

Why are Americans collaborating in a UN conspiracy to ruin South Africa with sanctions?

Newspaper column, 1986

Rail as they will against "discrimination," women are simply not endowed by nature with the same measures of single-minded ambition and the will to succeed in the fiercely competitive world of Western capitalism. The momma bird builds the nest. So it was, so it ever shall be. Ronald Reagan is not responsible for this; God is.

Newspaper column, 1983

I say Congress has an obligation to totally zero-out foreign aid, and cancel the $20 billion Mexican bailout, before it takes one penny out of the pockets of retired Americans who have paid Social Security taxes their entire lives. When I am elected president of the United States, there will be no more NAFTA sellouts of American workers. There will be no more GATT deals done for the benefit of Wall Street bankers. And there will be no more $50 billion bailouts of Third World socialists, whether in Moscow or Mexico City.

Announcement speech, 1995

Holier
Than Thou
That Old-Time Religion

Time was, Republicans didn't indulge in much public talk about their spiritual lives—they appear to have thought that religion was essentially a private matter. Abraham Lincoln, for example, never felt obliged even to announce what religion he was, and no one seemed interested in asking. Not any more. Religion is a campaign issue, and just about everyone has something to say about it.

The agenda Clinton & Clinton would impose on America—abortion on demand, a litmus test for the Supreme Court, homosexual rights, discrimination against religious schools, women in combat—that's change all right. But it is not the kind of change America wants. It is not the kind of change America needs. And it is not the kind of change we can tolerate in a nation we still call God's country...

PAT BUCHANAN, newspaper column, April 3, 1994

There is a religious war going on in this country for the soul of America. It is a cultural war, as critical as to the kind of nation we shall one day be as was the cold war itself. And, in that struggle for the soul of America, Clinton & Clinton are on the other side, and George Bush is on our side.

PAT BUCHANAN, quoting himself, newspaper column, May 11, 1994

I think in politics there are certain moral values. I'm one who—we believe strongly in separation of church and state, but then you get into some questions there are some

---

Two Old-Time Republican Presidents on Old-Time Religion

Leave the matter of religion to the family altar, the church, and private school, supported by private contributions. Keep the church and the state forever separate.

ULYSSES S. GRANT, 1875

I would rather be defeated than make capital out of my religion.

JAMES A. GARFIELD, 1880

---

moral overtones. Murder, that kind of thing, and I feel a little, I will say uncomfortable with the elevation of the religion thing.

GEORGE BUSH, explaining which side it is exactly that he's on, *Meet the Press*, September 16, 1984

I wouldn't say prayer, because then you ask, "What prayer?" I don't think there is any problem with a moment of silence. It's when most kids get to think of whether they remembered their shoes for the sixth-period gym class.

CHRISTINE TODD WHITMAN, Governor of New Jersey, on school prayer, 1995

And, yes, in the course of that vindication, we've created a fantastic economy. We have built up all kinds of materialistic strength. But you go back to the roots. You find what made it possible. And what made it possible was not a lot of junk about economics. What made it possible was that we stood from the beginning, on the belief, that our freedom comes from the Hand of God and must be exercised with respect and responsibility toward His existence and toward His will. That is the first principle of American life and American conservatism.

ALAN KEYES, February 23, 1996

Department of Utter Confusion

No, we don't know what they're talking about any more than they do, but you have our guarantee: These are all actual quotes.

It's only in the welfare state that we reduce things to their dumbest denominators.

> **NEWT GINGRICH**, *Meet the Press*, February 21, 1993

Let me suggest that I support the exceptions for rape, incest, life of the mother, and I would do pretty much as Bill, as Pat Buchanan indicates in this case. I want to make that clear; I thought we had just a short answer. But I wanted to underscore my strong pro-life record for people who have that view, and again, I think we can have different views and still be good Republicans.

> **BOB DOLE**, explaining his position on abortion,
> February 29, 1996

There's not much in either package to really jump-start the economy or blow it out of the water and make it really jump.

BOB DOLE, analyzing the differences between the Senate's economic plan and that of the Bush White House, 1992

High-tech is potent, precise, and in the end, unbeatable. The truth is, it reminds a lot of people of the way I pitch horseshoes. Would you believe some of the people? Would you believe our dog? Look, I want to give the high-five symbol to high-tech.

GEORGE BUSH, April 25, 1989

I don't know. I've never played a governor.

RONALD REAGAN, when asked during the 1966 California governor's campaign what kind of governor he would be

I don't know what these other guys are running for. I want to be President of the United States. I don't want an ad agency, never wanted an ad agency. I don't run a magazine. But I do know how to make Congress work. I know how to reach out to people. I know what the country needs. That's strong leadership. We need to defeat Bill Clinton.

BOB DOLE, trying to figure out what's going on February 29, 1996

I think there were some differences, there's no question, and will still be. We're talking about a major, major situation here... I mean, we've got a major rapport—relationship of economics, major in the security, and all of that, we should not lose sight of.

GEORGE BUSH, concerning trade talks with Japan
January 10, 1992

I don't know, my vision for America is to have a better America... I want a better life for your children. I want a better life, a better life, a better life than we had. We had a better life than our parents, our parents had a better life than their parents. That's what America's all about.

BOB DOLE, *The New York Times*, March 7, 1996

An Answer We're Glad the Interviewer Didn't Follow Up On

GEORGE WILL: Is this what the election is going to be about? Balanced budget? Is it about culture?

BOB DOLE: It's going to be about bad news.

The New York Times, March 7, 1996

How Did I Get Inside This Big White House, and Who Are All These People?

I can't tell until somebody tells me. I never know where I'm going.

RONALD REAGAN, when asked on Memorial Day in 1982 if he planned to visit the Vietnam Memorial

I am a man of limited talents from a small town. I don't seem to grasp that I am President.

WARREN G. HARDING, 1921

It gets into quota, go into numerical, set numbers for doctors or for, it could go into all kinds of things.

GEORGE BUSH on affirmative action programs, 1992

Part of the great success was the fact that we have an all-volunteer army, and part of the all—the military. And part of the rationale is people will have more say in what they want to do. So another—I want to be a part of this. I can respect that and understand it.

GEORGE BUSH, on women in the military, 1992

But that I'm out of touch with the American people, that I don't know people are hurting, I know it. I feel it. We pray about it, and I mean that literally at night, and, uh, many things, the various, where I don't care about, I don't know about education or don't, I mean, we've got a sound approach, innovative, revolutionary approach, and so I have to make it that clear.

GEORGE BUSH, on something or other, 1992

I'm just tossing this out… but maybe we need a tax credit for the poorest Americans to buy a laptop.

NEWT GINGRICH, 1995 congressional testimony

They Came From Outer Space

I've often wondered, what if all of us in the world discovered that we were threatened by an outer—a power from outer space, from another planet?

RONALD REAGAN, 1988

As people grow wealthier and the cost of space transportation comes down, spending a week's vacation on a space station or a honeymoon on the moon may become commonplace.

NEWT GINGRICH, *The Futurist*, June 1985

R. GENN

Military Matters, or Clinton the Draft-Dodging Wimp

Bob Dole is the only one of the Republicans most in the news these days who has had actual combat experience. Dornan and Lugar served during the 1950s in the peacetime armed forces, Lugar with, arguably, slightly more distinction. Buchanan, Keyes, Alexander, Gingrich, Gramm, Forbes—the Vietnam Era Republicans—did what most sensible college boys did back in those days: Dodged the draft for all they were worth, just like Clinton. But one of them might end up being Commander-in-Chief, so they all have to sound military.

You grow up an army brat named Newton and you learn something about combat.

NEWT GINGRICH, *Newsweek*, January 9, 1995

We have no defense. Why? Because a 20-year-old compact with a cheating Soviet regime, that has been dead half a decade, prevents us from building our missile defense. Well, that dereliction of duty ends the day I take the oath. I will maintain a military for the United States that is first on the land, first on the seas, first in the air, first in space—and I will not ask any nation's permission before I build a missile defense for the United States of America.

PAT BUCHANAN, announcement speech

Well, Because We Have Pilots Like Bob Dornan, That's Why

Why can't we buy just one airplane and have all the pilots take turns?

CALVIN COOLIDGE

In 1958, Dornan left active duty and joined the California Air National Guard as a fighter pilot and then the U.S. Air Force Reserve as a rescue and seaplane pilot and an intelligence officer, achieving the rank of captain. He survived two jet fighter emergency parachute ejections as well as two "dead stick" forced landings (F-100 jet fighter and H-13 solo helicopter).

BOB DORNAN, describing, in his campaign biography, his career as a fighter pilot. During slightly more than a year of flying—all of it during peacetime—Dornan managed to destroy two jet fighters, slamming one into a mountain, the other into the Pacific Ocean.

Marching As to War:
Exciting Realistic Combat Action
Starring Pat Buchanan

Pat Buchanan's actual experience of war is limited to watching John Wayne movies, so he is sometimes reduced to repeating second-hand war stories about his uncles. ("When I was a little boy, my four uncles went off to World War II. All four came home, but one uncle does not have a leg now—he has a Silver Star.") But more than any other Republican, he loves to talk war talk, any chance he gets:

Don't wait for orders from headquarters! Ride to the sound of the guns!

Speech, New Hampshire, February 20, 1996

That one went right down the smokestack on them!

The New York Times, March 3, 1996

The Bosnia of the cultural war is abortion.

Campaign position paper

This term limits movement has a whiff of revolution about it. We want to overthrow America's ruling class...

Speech, January 28, 1995

And as we defend our country from threats from abroad, we shall fight and win the cultural war for the soul of America.

Announcement speech, March 20, 1995

No matter how rich and prosperous we may become in material things, we cannot lose this battle for the heart and soul of America.

Announcement speech, March 20, 1995

To those Americans who have served this country in her wars from Europe to the Pacific, from Korea to Vietnam: This campaign is about you.

Announcement speech, March 20, 1995

The Washington Establishment was marching as to war and they were coming after me. The counterattack began then, and it continues to this day. Why? Because what we said at Houston went right down the smokestacks of America's cultural elite.

Christendom College speech, May 6, 1995

As we sacrificed and saved, and some of our friends fought and died, to win our war to preserve the body of Western Civilization, it is up to you to save her soul.

Christendom College speech, May 6, 1995

The Christian-bashers have made a major blunder. By laying down their artillery barrage five months before the off-year elections, they have exposed their position, revealed their tactics...

Speech, June 15, 1995

When I need a little advice about Saddam Hussein, I turn to country music.

GEORGE BUSH, October 21, 1991

The Citadel and V.M.I. should be allowed to remain all male. This arrangement preserves *esprit de corps*, maintains rigorous fitness standards for combat personnel, and keeps barracks life free from sexual distractions.

ALAN KEYES, campaign position paper, 1996

Bill Clinton continues to marginalize American power in the world. After winning the Cold War, this should not be America's fate. Our national security and our economic potential is based on America's strong leadership in the world.

RICHARD LUGAR, press release, June 5, 1995

I was shot down, and I was floating around in a little yellow raft, setting a record for paddling. I thought of my family, my mom and dad, and the strength I got from them. I thought of my faith, the separation of church and state.

GEORGE BUSH, speech about his war experiences, December 5, 1987

Oh, Say, Can You See
The Vision Thing

None of these Republicans is going to be tarred with the old "George-Bush-You've-Got-No-Vision" brush. These people have values galore and vision up the wazoo—and they're seeing things everywhere they go. Just listen to them:

I can see Georgia leading the way… I can see a country strong enough to defend itself… I can see a country proud enough and competitive enough… I can see a country that knows the difference between illegal immigration and legal immigration… I can see a country with schools that are as good as our colleges… I can see a country where the abortion rate and the divorce rate is headed down…

LAMAR ALEXANDER, February 29, 1996

I believe, I believe those of us in this room are the true sons and daughters I believe of the founding fathers. We are their legitimate and rightful heirs. We have never forgotten where we came from. Our heritage goes back to Lexington and Concord and Yorktown and Saratoga, and my friends in this campaign, we have conducted a three-week political campaign that will go down in legend in American political history.

PAT BUCHANAN, New Hampshire victory speech, February 20, 1996

Values mean returning to the inspiration of our forefathers that all of us are created equal. Values mean respecting parents enough to return control of the schools to them. That means giving parents the means to educate their children in the school of their choice. Values mean having a government that keeps its promises, like on Social Security and like working on a plan to provide for younger workers who now know they will get nothing. Values mean giving opportunity to all people by removing the red tape and taxes that suffocate our cities. Values mean welfare programs that help people rather than destroy them. Values mean real prison sentences for violent crimes. Values also mean refinding our moral compass in this world as a leader and light among nations, a U.N. foreign policy.

STEVE FORBES, campaign position paper, 1996

Hey! We got vision! We even got vision music!

BOB DOLE, hearing the sound track from *Star Wars* during a campaign stop, 1988

I have enormous personal ambition. I want to shift the entire planet. And I'm doing it. I am now a famous person.

NEWT GINGRICH, *The Washington Post*,
December 20, 1994

Richard Nixon was a man of vision, the largest figure of our time, whose influence will be timeless.

BOB DOLE, delivering the eulogy for Richard Nixon,
April 27, 1994

I see a different reality, an America of vast potential—greater than anything that has ever been seen before—waiting to be released. I see an American economy that is the most innovative and productive and technologically advanced in the world—hamstrung by high taxes and counter-productive regulations.

STEVE FORBES, announcement speech,
September 22, 1995

I believe that today, as throughout our history, most Americans want a President who will call on the better angels of our nature, and will unite the nation to face our common challenges head on. My vision for America sees a typical American family that actually enjoys better job prospects and more real income. Our paychecks will be bigger, our savings will be greater, and our hopes for the future will abound.

RICHARD LUGAR, announcement speech April 19, 1995

My vision for America is constant, constructive, hands-on American leadership in the world guided by presidential strength and wisdom.

RICHARD LUGAR, announcement speech, April 19, 1995

And it's great to be back in Iowa's state capital. These days I spend much of my time in another capitol. You see many things from atop the hill in Washington where I work—but you can see America from here.

BOB DOLE, announcement speech, April 11, 1995

Lamar Alexander: Plenty of Vision, but Not All of It 20/20

This is a long ride. And as I look all the way down the road, I see Dole running out of money, I see Dole not an executive leader, I see Dole without fresh ideas. I see us raising money, I see me with fresh ideas, I see me as an executive leader, and I see a Dole versus Alexander race that I can win.

LAMAR ALEXANDER, March 3, 1996

The Fair Sex
Republicans and Women

The Republicans don't differ among themselves all that much on the subject of women. They all quite sensibly try never to express their opinions on the subject in front of any women, however. They generally agree that abortion is a terrible idea under almost all circumstances, but there are some subtle differences, which we try to elucidate—in their own words—below.

The feminist agenda is not about equal rights for women. It is about a socialist, anti-family political movement that encourages women to leave their husbands, kill their children, practice witchcraft, destroy capitalism, and become lesbians.

> **PAT ROBERTSON**, fundraising letter quoted in *The Washington Post*, August 23, 1992

I know this is painful for the ladies to hear, but if you're married, you have accepted the headship of a man, your husband… Christ is head of the household, and the husband's the head of the wife and that's just the way it is… This is the way the Bible sets it up.

> **PAT ROBERTSON**, *The 700 Club* TV broadcast, January 8, 1982

All healthy societies understand that one of their primary goals is to train, educate, and acculturate young males.

The young males are the most dangerous physically, and they're the most dangerous in terms of being totally irresponsible. Because they are driven biologically to be nomadic, and to leave as many pregnant women behind as they can. And that's a biological reality.

NEWT GINGRICH, to an audience of Young Republicans, 1992

Abortion: The Subtly Different Views

I Want a Constitutional Amendment
Against It: PAT BUCHANAN, RICHARD LUGAR

I support a constitutional amendment that would overturn Roe v. Wade...

PAT BUCHANAN, Press release, January 30, 1996

I have also supported a constitutional amendment prohibiting abortion.

RICHARD LUGAR, campaign position paper, 1996

I'm With Ronald Reagan On that One,
Whatever He Said About It: PHIL GRAMM

First of all, let me say that I am pro-life. And we've got to have a Party that can bring together people... no matter how they stand on this issue, and there's no better role model for doing this than Ronald Reagan.

PHIL GRAMM, February 19, 1995

Well, It's Bad, but Not as Bad as Big Government: PAT BUCHANAN

The stand we ought to take is the stand taken by Ronald Reagan. He was pro-life all the way… he said, "Listen. This is what I believe and what I'm going to stand for. However, we've got to put together a 60 percent coalition so if you don't agree there on this issue, okay, do you agree with us on small government, strong defense? You're welcome to come in." That's the position I would take.

PAT BUCHANAN, February 19, 1995

The Intricate, and Somewhat Difficult-to-Follow, Biological Argument: ROBERT DORNAN

If you leave it alone and don't stop its heart and flatline its brainwaves, if you don't kill it, you can call it potential all you want, it is a human being. And we cannot avoid discussing this, in depth, in this race. Roe-Wade has given us 22 years of abortion on demand for any and all reasons or no reason at all through all 9 months.

ROBERT DORNAN, February 19, 1995

The Calm, Reasoned, Scholarly
Historical Perspective: ALAN KEYES

And we Republicans are going to have to decide again, as
we have had to decide in the past, whether we shall only
speak of justice and speak of principle or whether we shall
stand and fight for them! Whether we shall quote from the
words of the Declaration of Independence with real conviction or whether we shall take that document and throw it on
the ash heap of history as we adopt the message of those who
say that we can stand silent in the face of injustice! When it
comes to deciding whether we shall stand by the great principle that declares that all human beings are created equal
and endowed by their Creator with the right to life, there is
no choice for silence! There is no choice for silence!

ALAN KEYES, February 19, 1995

Let's Talk About Something Else,
Okay?: LAMAR ALEXANDER

The Federal Government should stay entirely out of it,
because I believe it's wrong and that states may restrict it.
I would characterize those views as pro-life. But I think we
need to move on, to other issues.

LAMAR ALEXANDER, February 19, 1995

Taxes
One More Thing All Republicans Can Agree On

Once more, total agreement. Vote for any of these guys, and you won't be paying any more of those annoying income taxes. Or if you are paying any, they'll be so much less annoying that you won't even notice.

Now is the time to kill the Taxasaurus monster! Kill the dinosaur, kill him now! If you don't, he's going to eat more jobs. So take this lead pencil and give him lead poisoning. Kill him!

AL D'AMATO, Senator from New York, in one of his more dignified moments, 1993

As president, I pledge to slash the federal tax burden on the American family by moving to a low flat income tax, and increasing the personal exemption for parents to $7,500 and children to $5,000 while retaining deductions for mortgage payments and charitable contributions.

PAT BUCHANAN, press release, December 5, 1995

The confiscatory inheritance tax now imposed on American family farms and small businesses is un-American. It is a dagger blow at the very heart of the American dream. The pioneers who came west and settled the rolling plains of Iowa pursued the great American dream of property ownership… When families work all their lives to save, purchase land, improve it, earn their keep from it and raise up their children on it, they have a moral right to hand it on to the next generation.

PAT BUCHANAN, *The Washington Times*, August 3, 1995

The rate is not the problem! The structure is not the problem! The tax itself is the problem! Abolish the income tax and restore the constitution of freedom under which this country was founded!

ALAN KEYES, February 29, 1996

To spur strong economic growth, America needs to balance the budget and eliminate the federal income tax. The IRS would be eliminated. A vastly smaller office or agency would be required to administer the national sales tax and the FICA tax. For most Americans, tax record keeping, audits, and the filing of forms would be things of the past.

RICHARD LUGAR, campaign position paper, 1996

Economics and History with Professors Buchanan and Coolidge, Second Semester

This [tariff] plan marries the growth ideas of Ronald Reagan to "The American System" devised by Hamilton and Washington, pursued by Jefferson and Lincoln, perfected by Theodore Roosevelt and Calvin Coolidge. That system converted America from a seaboard country of farmers into the mightiest industrial power on earth. America's giants blazed the trail and gave us the map; let us follow it.

PAT BUCHANAN, campaign position paper, 1996

The trouble with us is that we talk about Jefferson but do now follow him. In his theory that the people should manage their government, and not be managed by it, he was everlastingly right.

CALVIN COOLIDGE

Also-Rans
And You Thought the Left-Over Republicans Were Kind of Weak

Buchanan hung around a little before he realized his presidential candidacy was going nowhere. But here are some guys who, to paraphrase another famous Republican, we won't have to kick around any more. Too bad. They sure were a hoot when they were with us.

STEVE FORBES: Regular Guy

You probably think all Forbes has to say is "Flat tax! Flat tax! Flat tax!" followed by some percentage or other. Okay, in his abortive run for the nomination, the guy wasn't as quotable as Abraham Lincoln (or Robert Dornan), but when he finally got around to attacking Clinton, he managed to show some signs of life, even some modest degree of wit. So give the guy a break.

A dollar eighty-nine here, and $2.69 in New Jersey. It's $1.99 in New Hampshire.

STEVE FORBES, March 3, 1996, quoting the price of milk in South Carolina, New Jersey, and New Hampshire, and proving once and for all that he's just a regular guy like the rest of us, except that unlike the rest of us, he knows how much a gallon of milk costs in three different states. Or is that a half gallon?

When it comes to waffling, this man is the International House of Pancakes. We've been hearing a lot from the President about personal responsibility lately. And I'm all for that. But wouldn't it be nice if just once, just one time in his career, this President would honestly take responsibility for his own actions? Remember when he flip-flopped on the middle-class tax cut he promised during the 92 campaign, saying that if he cut taxes, the American people would only "waste the money." You do have to hand it to him, however. He ran on "change" in Washington, and then when he got to Washington, he changed his mind. I guess for this President, that's delivering on a promise.

Campaign position paper, 1996

ALAN KEYES: *The Only Republican Who Brags in His Campaign Biography That He Once Appeared on ABC's* Nightline

Alan Keyes' experience in government consists of being appointed to two positions under Reagan (Ambassador to the U.N. Economic and Social Council and Assistant Secretary of State for International Organizations), which explains why he wasn't in the papers much until he declared his candidacy for

R. GENN.

President. He's a very dramatic and compelling speaker, probably the only one besides Buchanan who doesn't induce somnolence. (Dornan can be exciting, but incoherent.)

We talk about leadership. Will somebody explain to me how we can expect Bob Dole to stand up to Bill Clinton and the Democrats when he can't even stand up to his own colleagues in the Senate to get our agenda through?

Quoted on the Alan Keyes Unofficial Internet Page

Whether you are choosing to have a baby out of wedlock or choosing to get an abortion, what is really wrong in that situation is that there is something deeply wrong with your moral compass and you need some help.

Quoted on the Alan Keyes Unofficial Internet Page

I favor abolishing the Department of Education. Federal grants and loans could be administered by Treasury or by a smaller, non-Cabinet-level agency. The federal role in higher education should be limited to promoting interests genuinely national in scope (e.g., education programs for military personnel).

Campaign position paper, 1996

RICHARD LUGAR: *You Can Wake Up Now. He's Done Talking.*

Richard Lugar may not be the most quotable politician out there, but when he gives a speech, he picks a topic and sticks to it—like Krazy Glue. With Perot's United We Stand, he went on at length about nuclear terrorism. With the Young Republicans, it was taxes and balanced budgets. But he is perhaps most distinguished for having given a speech to the Christian Coalition and only mentioned the word "Christian" five times—four times in the phrase "Christian Coalition" and once when referring to the Christian Science Monitor. Most of that speech concerned his principled opposition to legalized gambling. We couldn't find any evidence that any of the other candidates, or even the non-candidates, had any opinions whatsoever on legalized gambling, although we're sure they do, if only someone would ask. You may want to have someone take your pulse when you're done reading this section, just to make sure you haven't been bored to death.

Since my service on the Indianapolis Board of School Commissioners in the mid-60's, and continuing through my Senate career, I have supported voluntary school prayer. I was one of only 25 senators to support the Helms filibuster that was undertaken to restore an effective school prayer amendment to the Goals 2000 education bill.

Campaign position paper, 1996

I was the author of the anti-apartheid act in 1986. As Chairman of the Foreign Relations Committee, I brought about legislation that could pass both houses, and this particular unique instance, overcome the President Reagan's veto with a two-thirds majority. A sad occasion and the only time Reagan's veto was overcome. I had the voting record strongest for Reagan of all the people in the Senate, but ironically on this situation I felt the president had misread it, and I would simply say that I believe events in South Africa have vindicated that stand.

Speech, Montgomery County, Maryland June 20, 1995

The problem is that many Americans suspect that there is diminishing hope for a better future. The economic facts justify these beliefs. From 1950 through 1973, hourly compensation—including both wages and benefits—increased an average of 3.0 percent per year. Since 1973, the average wage increase has been less than one half of one percent. During the past two decades, economic growth has been cut in half, averaging only 2.4 percent annually. And if this isn't depressing enough for the average American family, limiting growth to 2.5 percent is the stated economic policy of the Federal Reserve Board. This we must change. The American public is demanding it.

Testimony to the House Ways and Means Committee, June 8, 1995

LAMAR ALEXANDER: *The One With the Howdy Doody Shirt*

When the campaign started, everyone was saying Lamar Who? And when he became the first to drop out of the race, they were still saying it. The first quote here pretty much sums up his gift for giving vivid form to the completely obvious.

Sooner or later, I need to begin to do what any candidate does in a presidential race. I need to begin to win…

I'm in this for the long haul. I have a long view. I mean, I'm the fellow who walked a thousand miles across Tennessee over six months when nobody thought it made any sense. I can go all the way to San Diego. My fund-raisers are prepared to do that, and my family is prepared to do that.

We have plenty of magazine salesmen. We got a lot of TV commentators. We have some excellent congressional leaders in Senator Dole and Newt Gingrich. That's not what we're lacking. What we're lacking is someone to give presidential leadership to the Republican agenda.

All quotes from *The New York Times*, March 4, 1996